EGYPT
GIFT OF THE NILE

DISCOVERING our HERITAGE

By Arthur Diamond

DILLON PRESS
New York

Maxwell Macmillan Canada
Toronto

Maxwell Macmillan International
New York Oxford Singapore Sydney

To Isadora and Leopold, and Ariane and Dan

Acknowledgments

The author would like to thank the following individuals who helped make this book possible: Leopold Gertler; Dan Hartstein; Dr. Lorena Siqueira; Nahed Gad of the Egyptian Tourist Authority in Chicago; Amira Kamel, press attaché of the Egyptian Embassy in Washington, D.C.; Ibrahim Hassan; Dr. Faoud Surur and Dr. Skina Surur; Abdulaleem El-Abyad and Mohamed Said of the Press and Information Bureau of the Permanent Mission of the Arab Republic of Egypt to the United Nations; Ben Burns; and my editor, Joyce Stanton.

Photographic Acknowledgments

Cover image courtesy of Dr. Lorena Siqueria

UN Photo 9, 16, 30-31, 56, 92-93; Abdulaleem El-Abyad 12-13, 22, 64, 80, 96, 103, 106, 109, 111; Dr. Lorena Siqueira 18, 43, 48-49, 60; Nahed Gad 36-37, 70-71, 74-75, 83, 87, 99; Nicholas Ghattas 114, 117

Library of Congress Cataloging-in-Publication Data

Diamond, Arthur.
    Egypt : gift of the Nile / by Arthur Diamond.
        p. cm. — (Discovering our heritage)
    Includes bibliographical references.
    Summary: Describes the land and people of Egypt, discussing both ancient and modern history, the geography, social life and customs, and folklore.
    ISBN 0-87518-511-8
    1. Egypt — Juvenile literature. [1. Egypt.] I. Title. II. Series.
DT49.D53 1992
962–dc20   91-43105

Dillon Press   Maxwell Macmillan Canada, Inc.
Macmillan Publishing Company   1200 Eglinton Avenue East
866 Third Avenue   Suite 200
New York, NY 10022   Don Mills, Ontario M3C 3N1

Macmillan Publishing Company is part of the Maxwell Communication Group of Companies.

First edition

Printed in the United States of America

10 9 8 7 6 5 4 3 2 1

Contents

Fast Facts about Egypt

Official Name: Jumhuriyyat Misr al-Arabiyyah (Arab Republic of Egypt).

Capital: Cairo.

Location: The northeastern corner of Africa.

Area: 386,662 square miles (1,001,449 square kilometers), which is roughly the size of Texas and New Mexico combined; it stretches 675 miles (1,086 kilometers) north to south, and 770 miles (1,240 kilometers) east to west; Egypt has 2,500 miles (4,000 kilometers) of coastline along the Mediterranean Sea, the Red Sea, the Gulf of Suez, and the Gulf of Aqaba.

Elevation: Highest — 8,668 feet (2,642 meters) at the peak of Mount Katherine, in the Sinai Peninsula; Lowest — 436 feet (133 meters) below sea level in the Qattara Depression, 300 miles (480 kilometers) west of Cairo.

Population: 55 million in 1991; about 96 percent of the country's entire population is concentrated in the 15,000 square miles (38,850 square kilometers) of land directly alongside the Nile River.

Form of Government: Republic. Head of Government — president. According to Egypt's constitution, only one person can run for president.

Important Products: Cotton, wheat, corn, iron ore, petroleum, and cement.

Basic Unit of Money: 1 Egyptian pound = 100 piasters.

Official Language: Arabic, with French and English spoken widely.

Religion: Islam is the official religion; fewer than 10 percent of the people are Coptic Christians.

Flag: The flag has horizontal red, white, and black stripes, with an eagle in the center.

National Anthem: "Belady, Belady" ("My Country, My Country").

Major Holidays: Eid al-Adha (time varies); Eid al-Fitr (following the Muslim month of Ramadan); Shem al-Nessim (the first Monday after the Coptic Easter).

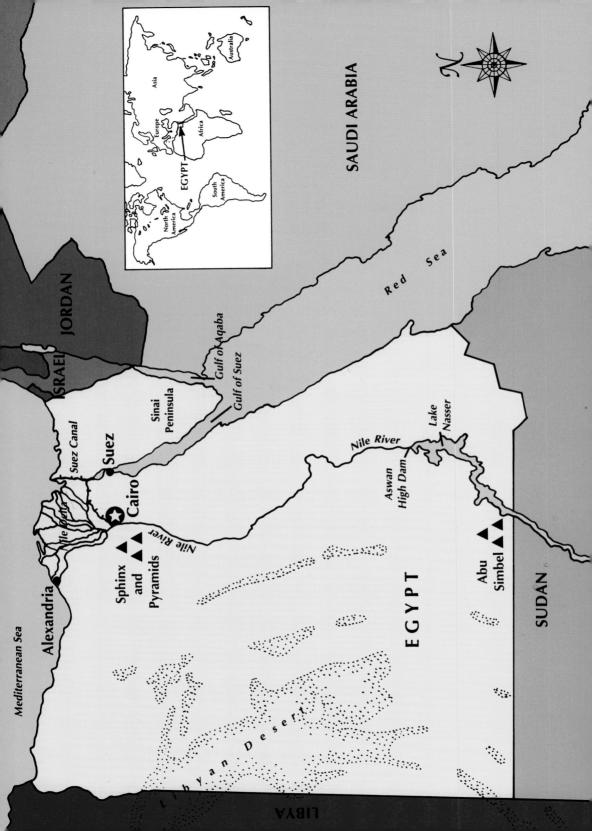

1. Victorious Egypt

With color and movement everywhere, busy Cairo often seems like a huge caravansary, or inn, for desert travelers. Shouting schoolchildren run up a street to meet with friends, while men and women in flowing robes and checkered headgear talk excitedly in the crowded *souks* (markets) and smoke-filled cafes. The shouts of street vendors and the squeal of automobile tires ring in your ears. The aromas of fried bread, *ful* (a national dish made of beans and spices), and mint tea mix with the powerful odors of trash and dung.

In Arabic, the name of this 1,000-year-old city is *al-Qahira,* or "victorious." One way to be "victorious" in this capital city of Egypt is to survive the heat and sand! Here, under the broiling sun, sights are blurred in waves of heat, and the taste in your mouth is sandy. There is sand everywhere, even between the pages of books in a person's apartment!

Besides the heat and sand, Egyptians have also struggled under the weight of foreign conquerors, cycles of drought and flood, and desperate poverty and disease. Yet Egypt endures. Its ancient monuments still stand, and its boundaries have remained relatively unchanged for thousands of years. Egypt's greatest victory is its continuing survival as a nation for such a long time — over 5,000 years! Egypt and its people have certainly been victorious — over heat and sand, and also over time.

A Desert Nation

Egypt is at the northeastern corner of the continent of Africa. It covers an area of 386,662 miles (1,001,449 square kilometers) — about the size of New Mexico and Texas combined. You could say that Egypt is jug-shaped, with the Sinai Peninsula to the east attached like a handle. The Suez Canal — a famous waterway that connects the Mediterranean and Red seas — separates the peninsula from the rest of Egypt. Large freighters and ships, as well as Egyptian sailboats, called *feluccas,* cruise through the canal.

Egypt's border to the north is the Mediterranean Sea. Throughout history, sailors and explorers have crisscrossed the Mediterranean in search of new wealth and adventure. Egypt's delta area — the triangle of land where the Nile River runs into the sea — has been deeply influenced by the various groups of people arriving from other Mediterranean countries, like Italy, Greece, and Turkey.

To the east lies the Red Sea and its arms, the Gulf of Suez and the Gulf of Aqaba. These gulfs are on either

A crowded souk *in Cairo, where you can buy everything from food and clothing to handmade pottery, brass objects, and colorful rugs.*

side of the Sinai Peninsula. The Red Sea itself is usually blue-green in color, but it sometimes turns reddish brown when the tiny plants in it, called algae, die. The sea is a popular fishing and resort area for Egypt and also for Israel, which borders the Sinai Peninsula in the northeast.

The Nile River cuts through Egypt, leaving desert regions to the east and west. The Arabian Desert lies alongside the Red Sea. Unlike the other desert regions of Egypt, it is often mountainous. Here you will find the nation's highest peak, Mount Katherine, on the Sinai Peninsula.

Desert extends to Egypt's borders in the west and the south. The Libyan Desert, with its sparse vegetation and blinding sandstorms, covers nearly 70 percent of the country — from the Nile Valley west to Libya and from the Mediterranean coast in the north to the republic of Sudan in the south. The desert regions are populated only by nomadic tribes that have learned to survive in the harsh environment. In some parts of the Egyptian desert, though, you will find an oasis.

The Oasis

An oasis is an area of water and plant life in the middle of a desert. Oases are green because they get water from underground streams. El Faiyum, an oasis in the Libyan Desert 90 miles (145 kilometers) southwest of Cairo, is also one of Egypt's finest resorts. With its groves of almond, orange, and fig trees, as well as its vineyards, El Faiyum dazzles the eyes of all who come here. There is even a lake crowded with fish! In ancient times, El Faiyum was known as the Garden of Egypt.

Farther to the south are the Kharijah and Dakhilah oases. Bountiful fields and lakes, as well as the remains of temples and fortresses, are found at both oases. Kharijah, also known as the Great Oasis, is the largest in Egypt: It stretches about 200 miles (322 kilometers) from end to end! Dakhilah is Egypt's most densely populated oasis.

The Nile, Egypt's "Tree of Life"

While Egypt is a crowded country, the population is not spread out evenly over the land. More than 55 million people live in Egypt, and most of them are crowded within one long, narrow stretch of land ranging from 1/2 mile to 12 miles (.80 to 20 kilometers) wide. This is the area that lies along both sides of the Nile River. The waters of the Nile make the nearby land fertile. Beyond this narrow strip of green are miles and miles of desert.

The Nile is Egypt's only river. Satellite photos show that it looks like an upside-down tree, with its "trunk" stretching toward Sudan and its "roots," or delta, spreading into the Mediterranean. Indeed, we can

The ancient Nile winds through modern Cairo.

call the Nile Egypt's "tree of life," because life here depends on it so much. The Greek historian Herodotus said that Egypt itself is "the gift of the Nile."

The Nile is also the longest river in the world — it runs for over 4,000 miles (6,440 kilometers). It starts far away in the south, in the mountains of Tanzania, another African country. In Egypt, it flows for 960 miles (1,546 kilometers), from Upper Egypt to Lower Egypt.

You would naturally think that Upper Egypt would be in the north of the country, but it's not. The Nile flows from the higher ground in the southern part of the country to the low delta area in the north, finally emptying into the Mediterranean Sea.

The climate along the Nile, as elsewhere in Egypt, is mostly hot and dry. Summer lasts from May to October and brings temperatures of between 80 and 110°F (27 and 43°C). In the winter months, from November to April, the temperature ranges from 55 to 70°F (13 to 21°C). Temperatures have been known to drop even lower, though. Occasionally, Egyptians in the temperate delta region wake up to find light frost on the ground!

Upper Egypt

Upper Egypt is mostly desert, with the Nile cutting a path through sand and dry, rocky valleys. Some 435 miles (700 kilometers) to the south of Cairo is the Aswan High Dam. Completed in 1970 and located 5 miles (8 kilometers) south of the city of Aswan, the dam has changed the course of life for Egyptian farmers. For thousands of years, they depended upon the river's annual floods, which deposited fertile soil, or silt, along the valley and on the delta. The dam ended the yearly floods and trapped the surplus waters in Lake Nasser, the 300-mile- (483-kilometer-) long lake that formed behind the dam. Without the rich soil deposits, farmers in the Nile Valley need to use more artificial fertilizers on their land. But the high dam has been able to improve the life of the farmers by providing them with electricity and a steady flow of water that is used for irrigation.

Lower Egypt

Cairo marks the unofficial border between Upper and Lower Egypt. North of Cairo, in Lower Egypt, the Nile begins to widen into a delta, which is the fan-shaped mouth of a river where it meets the sea. Here, the Nile forks into two main channels: the Rosetta to the west and the Damietta to the east. Both forks create the delta, the piece of land that spreads out in a great triangle reaching over 150 miles (241 kilometers) at its base, where the river empties into the Mediterranean Sea.

Nutrient-rich mud washing slowly downriver builds
up the Nile Delta, making it one of the most fertile
regions in the world. Traveling north from Cairo, you
will begin to see large fields of cotton, maize (corn), and
rice, as well as men working beside their grazing sheep,
donkeys, and water buffalo. You will also find many
small towns and villages: The Nile Delta is one of the
most densely populated rural areas in the world.

Once there was much wildlife in the Delta. Hun-
dreds of varieties of fish and colorful birds made the

marshy land their home. Crocodiles and hippopota-
muses ruled the water. Gazelles, boars, and wildcats
roamed the riverbanks. Asps and horned vipers slithered
among the papyrus, a plant that still grows up to nine
feet tall along the river. But the vast numbers of people
now crowded into the area have made fish and other
wildlife rare. Only 300 kinds of birds remain in the
entire country today.

Industry

Nearly half of all Egyptians are farmers. They work
either on their land or that of someone else. Other Egyptians find jobs in factories that manufacture machinery,
fertilizer, cement, and steel. Some work in mines, where
they dig for gypsum and iron ore. Some find jobs in
banking.

Despite the fertility of the Nile Delta, Egypt must
import even its most essential food products in order to
feed its great population. For example, wheat is used
everywhere in Egypt to make bread. But Egyptian farmers can't grow enough of this grain, so the United States
provides most of it. Other food products, which include
beans, corn, clover, potatoes, millet, rice, onions, and
sugarcane, are never plentiful.

One important reason why Egyptian farmers cannot
grow sufficient food crops is that large tracts of land are

*The water trapped by the Aswan High Dam is used to irrigate
more than a million acres of farmland.*

needed to raise the nation's most important crop, cotton. Egypt is among the world's top producers of cotton. And it leads all countries in the production of high-quality, long-fibered cotton. Some 70 percent of its cotton is exported. Egypt's export trade developed during the American Civil War to supply the British textile industry. Britain was cut off from American cotton by the Union blockade of Southern ports. Cotton, or "white gold," as it came to be called, greatly strengthened Egypt's economy in the 1860s.

While cotton continues to be important to Egypt's economy, today oil and tourism bring in most of the nation's money. Fees paid by ships passing through the 100-mile- (161-kilometer-) long Suez Canal help, too. Also, Egyptians working in other countries send money home. Many villagers look to Egypt's cities for opportunity.

Egypt's Cities

Alexandria is Egypt's famous port city. Located on the shore of the Mediterranean, it has a population of nearly six million and is the nation's second-largest city. In ancient times, around 200 B.C., Alexandria was a renowned center of culture and learning. Its library, which housed more than 700,000 scrolls, drew scholars from all over the world. Unfortunately, this valuable

Almost half of all Egyptians work the land.

collection has not survived. In modern times, the city became a leading commercial center. It attracted bright, ambitious foreigners and was often called the "Oriental Paris." Men from Turkey, Greece, and other countries in the Mediterranean region went there to work in banks or to be traders, shippers, or manufacturers. Today, Alexandria can boast of its ancient glory, sandy beaches, and the nation's largest modern library: The Alexandria University Library contains over one million books.

Egypt's true center, however, is Cairo, the capital city. From the air, Cairo is a huge, sprawling city of circling avenues, its buildings and houses the same color as the desert sand that surrounds them. With the famous Giza pyramids, the Sphinx, and the Nile flowing through it, Cairo is the largest city in Africa. It is four times as large as the next-largest city, Lagos, Nigeria.

To look at Cairo's buildings is to be struck by the contrasts of East and West, rich and poor. The wrought-iron balconies of older European-style apartment buildings face new *mosques* (Muslim houses of worship), their *minarets,* or spires, pointing to the sky. The former homes of wealthy Europeans contrast with the rows and rows of old, flat buildings divided into one-room apartments. These have no electricity and no running water. They are rented by the droves of poor villagers moving in from the countryside.

Cairo is overflowing with people. The streets are difficult to walk through. The buses that speed down the avenues are packed on the inside and dotted on the outside with men and boys hanging on for dear life. The markets are busy at all hours of the day. Although the city's population was recently estimated at about eight million, more than 14 million people might actually live there. So many poor Cairenes — crowded into so many buildings and houses — lead invisible lives: They are never counted by the government.

Egypt's Government

Egypt became a republic in 1953. Today its official name is the Arab Republic of Egypt. But for a number of years, in an effort to unite the Arab world, the country called itself the United Arab Republic. This was the result of an alliance Egypt made with Syria in 1958. Although the union lasted only three years, Egypt kept the title until 1971.

Under Egypt's constitution, adopted in 1971, a president heads the government. He is nominated by one-third of the members of the legislature, called the People's Assembly, and is approved by two-thirds of that body. He is then elected by referendum, or popular vote. Since there is no opposition candidate, the people

can only vote their approval of him. The president serves six years at a time and may be reelected an unlimited number of times.

According to law, the People's Assembly must be made up of not less than 350 members, each elected by the people for six years. Half of them must be workers or farmers, and a certain percentage of them must be female. The president is allowed to appoint up to ten additional members.

Egypt's form of government is called a "socialist democracy," which implies that it is a democracy that considers the rights of working people most important. However, the constitution is not always followed. The president actually has enormous authority. He is able to control the press and even manipulate elections to maintain power while giving the appearance of democracy.

An elaborate gateway marks the entrance to the Khan El-Khalili bazaar in Cairo.

2. *The Enduring Egyptians*

Finding the "average" Egyptian is not as simple as it would seem, because people have come to Egypt from many different lands. Also, life in one part of the country can differ greatly from life in another part. However, Egyptians can be grouped according to the length of time they have been in Egypt.

The "new" Egyptians are recent immigrants. Some have come from Europe, but most are from Arab countries, such as Syria, Lebanon, and Jordan. They usually live in Egypt's cities, where they find established communities willing to help them find jobs and housing.

Many Egyptians are of "older" stock. Their forebears came as members of conquering armies. Egypt is one of the few Arab countries that has long-standing borders, but these borders have been crossed many times by foreigners, and one can find Egyptians of Turkish, Greek, Italian and, of course, Arabic origin. These people, whose ancestors immigrated over the course of more than 2,000 years, also live mostly in the cities, where many prosper in business and the professions.

In the rural areas, one finds the most well-established Egyptians. They are made up of three groups: the Nubians, the *Bedouin,* and the *fellahin.* The Nubians, a dark-skinned people originally from Sudan, have lived for thousands of years along the Nile River in Upper Egypt, beyond the Aswan High Dam. The Bedouin, on the other hand, keep away from the river. They are animal herders who for centuries have moved from place to place across the great desert expanses seeking fresh pastureland. They live on the meat and dairy products of their camels, goats, and sheep.

The Fellahin

The fellahin make up the third major group of well-established Egyptians. They are perhaps most representative of today's average Egyptian. "Fellahin" is the Arabic name for the peasant farmers who live and work in Nile villages as their forebears have for 50 centuries. The fellahin make up about half of the total population of Egypt.

The fellahin have to cope with primitive living conditions. For thousands of years — and right up to the present day — the fellahin have trudged barefoot through the waters of the Nile and over its soggy banks, driving oxen and planting grain. Wearing their traditional robes as protection against the blazing sun, they strain their muscles

The ancient Egyptian waterwheel, or sakieh, *is still being made today.*

working primitive tools like the Archimedes' screw. Archimedes, a Greek scientist, invented this device 200 years before the birth of Christ. It is basically a huge corkscrew in a tube used to lift water from the Nile.

Another ancient tool still used today by the fellahin is the *sakieh,* a large wheel to which several buckets are attached. A small boy rotates the sakieh as he rides a blindfolded water buffalo, ox, or camel, which walks in a circle. The movement of the animal makes the buckets empty their contents into a ditch, which is part of the irrigation system.

The fellahin work hard. Sometimes they work after dark and through the night, laboring steadily beneath the light of the moon. Usually, though, they return in the evening to their villages.

The fellahin have had to get used to living almost shoulder-to-shoulder with their neighbors. Fellahin live in mud-brick houses set very close to one another, separated only by narrow alleys. In the villages, everything is close together so that all available fertile soil can be cultivated.

The fellahin's simple pleasures are few. When not exhausted from work, they like to spend time with their families or visit friends. Occasionally they go to the souk or enjoy a cup of coffee at a cafe. After dinner, a father will bring his male children with him to the local mosque for prayers. His wife and daughters remain in their house to pray. Afterward, everyone is reunited at home, where they go to sleep early to rest for the next strenuous day.

Egyptian Pride and Friendship

Many Egyptians are plagued by the problems of over-crowding, poverty, and disease, and they must also battle feelings of despair. Yet they survive. Certain distinctive traits — pride, humility, a good sense of humor, and piety — seem to help all Egyptians cope and endure.

As the nation's population grows by more than one million people every year, Egyptians must cope with terrible living conditions. Houses are in such short supply that many people are forced to live in the streets, especially in the cities. In Cairo, where entire families live on the sidewalks, there is a graveyard called the City of the Dead. Here, poor people live among and inside houselike tombs, where they find shelter from the hot sun as well as places to store their few belongings. Although they lack a sewage system and have only a few communal water taps, they keep their surroundings organized and clean. And they often share what they have with other poor families. Some of these squatters say, in fact, that life in the City of the Dead is better than life on the streets of downtown Cairo.

Those Cairenes fortunate enough to have apartments take pride in the cleanliness and order of their dwellings. In this city where most buildings look as if they are about to fall down or fall apart, a visitor steps into another world when he or she enters a person's apartment. The outside of the building and its lobby may be cracked and peeling, but each apartment is kept neat and orderly.

Friendship is vital to Egyptians, and the souk is a favorite place to gather. Souks are almost always colorful, crowded, and noisy. In this lively atmosphere, people bargain over handmade pottery, colorful rugs, shiny brass objects, clothing, and food. Most of all, it is here that Egyptians love to talk. Old friends delight in debating controversial issues, sharing opinions, or just plain gossiping. Students hotly discuss politics while selling dried fruits and nuts to shoppers. Egyptians say that arguing keeps people from really getting mad at each other!

Friends also get together at the cafe. *Ittfadel,* the men say, which means "welcome" or "help yourself." Coffee is prepared in three ways, according to the amount of sugar added to it: *ziyada* (sweet), *mazboota* (medium), or *saada* (bitter). At a cafe a man might interrupt conversation to smoke from a hookah. A hookah, or water pipe, carries hot tobacco smoke through a chamber filled with cool water to a rubber tube with a mouthpiece. The cooled smoke is then inhaled, giving the smoker relief from the harsh tastes and smells of daily life. The pipes are rented for various lengths of time and passed from man to man.

Cairo's trash collectors, the zabbaleen, make their early morning rounds on donkey cart.

Other Distinctive Traits

We can say that Egyptians also have the distinctive traits of humility, solidarity, courtesy, and compassion. Their sense of humility, for example, reveals itself in many instances. To help bring in money for the family, the children often must work with their parents, whatever their parents do. In Cairo, some boys rise at dawn to go to work with their fathers on garbage carts to collect trash. These *zabbaleen,* or garbage collectors, receive no pay, but they get to keep the garbage and sell the recycled trash. They may be lowly workers, but they are determined and proud. Unfortunately, they earn very little money for their recycled trash.

After enduring centuries of foreign rule, Egyptians have developed a strong sense of solidarity. So it was no surprise when former President Anwar el-Sadat expelled advisers from the Soviet Union in 1972. This action not only improved relations with the United States, but also pleased Egyptian citizens, who resented the presence of the Soviets. Many Egyptians are sympathetic to the old Arab saying: "I and my brothers against my cousins, I and my cousins against my tribe, and I and my tribe against the world."

While they do not like to be dominated by foreigners, the Egyptians display a strong sense of courtesy to strangers. The Bedouin, for example, always treat strangers extremely well. When visitors arrive, the

Bedouin men may slaughter a lamb for a special meal. The women cook the meat, but they do not share in the feast. In keeping with Bedouin tradition, they wear black veils and remain a respectful distance from strangers.

Compassion, too, is an Egyptian trait. An interesting example of this occurred after Egypt's 1967 war with Israel. Egyptian President Gamal Abdel Nasser's forces suffered a humiliating defeat. Yet, when the dejected leader went before his people to offer his resignation, throngs of supporters cheered him and refused to allow him to leave. They recognized his suffering and humiliation, just as if it were their own.

Traditional Dress

Many Egyptians have pride in their culture and see no reason to change their traditional ways of dress. Both in the cities and in rural areas, men wear *gallabiyyas,* which are flowing gowns, usually white, and resemble nightshirts. They are ideal for the climate, whether hot or cold, because they both reflect the sun and retain the cooler body heat. On their heads many men wear a *fez,* also called a *libdeh,* which protects them from the sun's burning rays.

In rural areas, everyone wears traditional clothing. Many women wear black, hooded robes, called *milayah,* as well as dresses with more colorful designs. These designs are distinctive to each village. Some enterprising Egyptians have borrowed the patterns to create dresses for shops in the cities, so that women from all over the country can share in their heritage.

Although they are in the minority, many Egyptians are attracted to nontraditional clothing. In the cities, women and girls often wear Western fashions, and many men wear Western-style pants and jackets. At the beach, some women and girls even wear bikinis, like foreign visitors.

Religion

Islam, which means "submission," is the religion of Egypt. Islam claims some 90 percent of all Egyptians as *Muslims,* or "ones who submit." Muslims submit to God (or in Arabic, *Allah*) their one and only god. A holy man named *Muhammad,* born in the city of Mecca in Saudi Arabia, was the founder of Islam about 1,400 years ago.

Islam, a vital part of the average Egyptian's daily life, requires strict obedience. Its followers must pray five times a day, facing the direction of Mecca. The *muezzin,* or crier, calls to the faithful to come to prayer: "*Allahu akbar* (God is most great)*! La ilaha illa Allah* (There is no god but God)*! Al-salat khayr min al-naum* (Prayer is better than sleep)!"

The muezzin calls from a minaret, a tower of the mosque, which is the building where Muslims pray.

When the faithful Muslims hear the call, they stop what they are doing—whatever they are doing—to pray. At this time, all of Cairo's cars and trucks and buses screech to a halt. Drivers and passengers climb out of their vehicles, face east toward Mecca, and kneel on the ground.

A journey, or pilgrimage, to Mecca is the high point of a Muslim's life. Muslims from all over the world try to make the journey at least once in their lives. Egyptians who have gone to the holy city proudly paint the outsides of their houses with colorful scenes from their pilgrimages.

Some 7 to 10 percent of Egypt's population are members of the Coptic Orthodox Church. The Copts are descended from ancient Egyptians who were converted to Christianity in the second and third centuries after Christ. They take their name from a Greek word meaning "Egyptians." Unlike other Christians who believe that Christ was both human and divine, Copts believe only in Christ's divinity.

Before the Muslims conquered Egypt in A.D. 642 and converted many Christians to Islam, the Copts were the majority religion in Egypt. Today they add to the color and richness of Egyptian culture. Walking through the streets of Cairo today you might come across Christian celebrations, with festive lights and pictures of Jesus and Mary. Copts often have a small cross tattooed on their wrists, and they hold jobs in government, military, and business.

A quiet beauty marks the oldest mosque in Egypt, the Amr Ibn El-Aas.

There are also some synagogues in Egypt, since a small Jewish community still lives there. The largest Jewish community is in Alexandria, though most of Egypt's Jews now live across the border in Israel.

Culture

Egyptians consider their nation the leader of the Arab world in matters of culture. Egypt's press is noted for its wide range of political expression, something unusual in the Middle East, and Egyptians are very proud of this. Also, Egyptians claim — and rightly so — that Cairo is the publishing capital of the Arab world. The city produces and distributes books, newspapers, and magazines to other Arab countries.

Books are especially valued by Egyptians. One who can read and discuss a subject intelligently is one who is respected. At school, children learn about Egyptian writers such as Taha Hussein. Hussein was one of modern Egypt's leading authors. He supervised the translation of Shakespeare into Arabic and wrote many novels and essays. He died in 1973. In 1988, another Egyptian writer, Naguib Mahfouz, won the Nobel Prize for literature. He has written over 30 novels about life in modern Egypt and is finally becoming known here in the West.

Like all Arab-speaking people, Egyptians love poetry. While schoolchildren are required to study it, older Egyptians like to memorize poetry so that they can entertain the many people who cannot read or write. From time immemorial, reciting poems has been a favorite way to amuse and educate the people.

Egyptians also enjoy music. In old quarters (neighborhoods) of Cairo and Alexandria, musical instruments are made by hand and are very popular. A laborer, for example, finds the flute easy to carry and soothing to play as he heads out to work in the fields. Small harps are played by the workers, too. At night, strolling musicians entertain crowds in the streets of the villages and cities, and they encourage their listeners to dance.

Dance has always had a great following in Egypt. The children like Western-style dancing and rock and roll, while ballet is preferred by the older generations. However, belly dancing is popular with all.

Belly dancing is a studied skill, viewed by both sexes. The important movements take place around the belly and the hips. The belly dancer, dressed in a sheer costume and adorned with jewelry, often accompanies her dance with finger cymbals. An orchestra of perhaps 20 musicians may also accompany her. Egyptians appreciate belly dancing as part of their cultural heritage, and tourists love to watch it, too.

Movies and Museums

Egypt was once known as the Hollywood of the Middle East. In the 1940s, Cairo produced over 50 movies a year, and in the following decade, that number rose to 70. Egyptians flocked to the theaters to see their favorite Egyptian and American films. Then came Nasser's regime in 1952, bringing with it a restructuring of the studio system, and the production of films fell. The movie industry got much smaller. Today, despite rising costs, competition from video films, and a diminishing audience, Cairo's movie industry still dominates the Middle East.

Egyptians are proud of their country's achievements. The Egyptian Museum, founded in 1857, is one of many institutions showing off the nation's great past. Mummies and ancient tools and jewelry dazzle the eye in a beautiful display. There is also a post-office museum, as well as a cotton museum, a railroad museum, and several religious museums. In the Agricultural Museum in Cairo, you can see 5,000-year-old samples of flat and raised breads, seeds, and garments! They have all been remarkably preserved in the dry desert air of the tombs.

Many foreigners have the idea that Egypt is merely a museum, crowded with lifeless artifacts from a distant time. But Egypt is truly a dynamic land buzzing with the vitality of its people.

3. Many Conquerors Through Time

An Egyptian intellectual once described the rest of the Arab world as simply "tribes with flags." This is because most countries in the Middle East never had definite boundaries. Today's map of that part of the world was drawn up by Britain and France after World War I.

Egypt, along with Iran, is one of the few countries in the Middle East with historical boundaries. Within these boundaries, though, Egypt has been ruled by various foreigners for long periods throughout history.

Over 8,000 years ago, wandering tribes in northeastern Africa settled down and began what was to become one of the greatest civilizations in the world. The primitive Nile Valley hunters, thought to have long heads and dark, wavy hair, were joined in 6000 B.C. by broad-headed wanderers, probably from the area to the east that was later known as Palestine.

By 3600 B.C. these settlers were working together and growing figs, dates, and beans. They stored all their foods as well. They wove cloth, used copper utensils, and lived in homes of brick and straw.

A Nation Is Born

The early Egyptians gradually formed themselves into small states. Over time, these merged into two large states, Upper Egypt and Lower Egypt. Lower Egypt consisted of the Nile Delta. Upper Egypt included territory south of the delta on both sides of the Nile. Around 3100 B.C. a king arose in Upper Egypt who conquered Lower Egypt and formed one kingdom. Menes, as he was known, founded the first Egyptian dynasty — a series of rulers in the same family. He established his capital at Memphis, near present-day Cairo.

Menes's dynasty and the one that followed his ruled Egypt for about 400 years. During this period, the people developed a national government. They created a new style of architecture and began to use writing. Farmers learned how to irrigate their fields and began to use the plow. Craftsmen developed metal tools such as axes and knives.

The Old Kingdom

During the period from 2700 B.C. to 2200 B.C., Egyptians made their greatest achievements in art and architecture. Under the direction of their powerful kings, who were believed to be gods, Egyptians built more than 20 major pyramids. This Age of the Pyramids ended in

More than 4,000 years ago, the Sphinx and the great Pyramid of Cheops were built at Giza, near present-day Cairo.

confusion, however, as the kings lost power to several ambitious local rulers.

The First Intermediate Period

For about 150 years (2200–2050 B.C.) rival families competed for the throne, and Egypt endured political and social chaos. Civil wars brought misery to the people. Trade declined. The arts suffered.

The Middle Kingdom

It took a group of nobles from Thebes, a city 300 miles (483 kilometers) south of Cairo, to reunite the land. During the period of the Middle Kingdom, from 2050–1800 B.C., a strong ruler came to power, King Amenemhet III. He resumed trade with other countries and gradually extended Egypt's influence south into Nubia and east into Palestine and Syria.

The Second Intermediate Period

After 1800 B.C., a series of weak kings again allowed local princes to regain some of their independence. As these nobles competed for power, the nation was weakened and left exposed to foreign invaders. The Hyksos, a people from the area of Palestine, gradually conquered

Egypt in the 1700s B.C. They had the advantage of new tools of war. They introduced the horse and chariot, new types of bronze weapons, and body armor. They dominated Egypt for about a century.

The Early New Kingdom

By 1570 B.C. the Egyptians, having learned how to use the new weapons, drove the Hyksos out and restored peace. Under Queen Hatshepsut, Egypt entered a new era of peace and prosperity. The queen sent trading expeditions to various parts of Africa. Preferring arts to warfare, she built many beautiful temples and palaces.

The queen's peaceful policy ended with the rule of Thutmose III, her successor. Under his forceful leadership, the Egyptian Empire achieved its greatest size. He conquered Lebanon, Palestine, Syria, and much of the Nile Valley. He created a colonial administration that helped Egypt hold its widespread possessions for a century.

During the period of the Early New Kingdom, which lasted until 1300 B.C., an extraordinary king arose. Amenhotep IV, who came to the throne about 1370 B.C., worshiped the sun. He developed a religion that was close to monotheism, a belief in one god. He called the sun Aton and changed his own name to Akhenaton. He prohibited his people from worshiping more than one god, and forced them to worship him as a god-king and as the son of Aton. During Akhenaton's reign, Egyptians began calling their king "pharaoh."

The Egyptian people did not easily accept their pharaoh's beliefs. And because he was more concerned with affairs at home, the country's outlying possessions revolted. Under King Tutankhamen, the Egyptians returned to their old religious practices of worshiping many gods.

The Later New Kingdom

The period of years marked by the Later New Kingdom, from 1300 to 1090 B.C., saw Egyptians recover their empire in Asia and their leadership in trade and commerce. But they had to fight two powerful groups of people. The Philistines threatened Egypt with invasion from the eastern Mediterranean Sea. The Hittites fought the Egyptians on land in Asia.

Egypt eventually lost its powerful role in the ancient world. While other civilized nations developed iron tools, Egypt had no sources of this metal and found it difficult to import it from Asia. Egypt was rich in copper, and while that metal was essential, Egyptians could dominate the region. Now Egypt could not compete with armies that had iron weapons. Gradually, Egypt lost its empire. The once-mighty nation declined into a number of small states that traded with each other but competed for political power.

The Period of Invasions

The weakened, divided nation was now exposed to foreign invaders. Non-Egyptians would dominate the land for centuries. The period of invasions began with a Libyan prince, who seized the Egyptian throne around 945 B.C. He was followed some 200 years later by a Sudanese leader, who overthrew the Libyans. Some 85 years after that event, the Assyrians conquered the land.

By 525 B.C., the Persians had driven out the Assyrians. They ruled the country for about 200 years. In 332 B.C., Alexander the Great added Egypt to his empire. The famous young conqueror built up a port on the Mediterranean and named it Alexandria, after himself. He brought Greek ideas and the Greek way of doing things to Egypt. When he died, in 323 B.C., he left a new dynasty in charge of Egypt.

Ptolemy, one of Alexander's leading generals, took the title of King of Egypt in 306 B.C. and founded the dynasty known as the Ptolemies. The Ptolemies developed Egypt's resources and culture. They made Alexandria the national capital. Under their rule, Alexandria

became the intellectual and religious center of the world. The dynasty of the Ptolemies lasted nearly 300 years. It ended with the death of its last ruler, the famous Cleopatra, in 30 B.C.

Although not especially beautiful, Cleopatra was intelligent, witty, and ambitious. She attracted some of the greatest Romans of her day. Her love affairs with Julius Caesar and Mark Antony have been the subject of literary masterpieces down through time.

Perhaps because the Ptolemies developed Egypt so well, the Romans became interested in it. In 30 B.C., their armies conquered the country and made it a Roman province. Egypt was under Roman control for some 400 years. Around A.D. 395, the Roman Empire split into eastern and western sections. The East Roman Empire was called Byzantium, and Egypt was a Byzantine province until the Arabs conquered the land in A.D. 642.

Rise of Islam

Under Roman and Byzantine rule, many Egyptians had been converted to Christianity. But the Arabs brought Islam, a new religion, to the people they conquered. The Arabs spread the teachings of the prophet Muhammad throughout the Middle East and North Africa. They made Egypt a province, called a *caliphate,* of the Arab empire.

(Previous pages) Four colossal statues of Ramses II, who ruled from about 1290 to 1224 B.C., guard one of the temples at Abu Simbel.

With the coming of the Mamelukes, Egypt went through a violent period. The Mamelukes ("military slaves") were originally non-Arab slaves acting as bodyguards for Egypt's rulers. They managed to take over the government of Egypt in 1250. They ruled for more than 250 years. Though this period saw high achievements in literature and architecture, the Mamelukes controlled the country with cunning and ruthlessness. In 1517, the Mamelukes were overthrown by the Ottoman Turks. In that year, the last Mameluke leader, Tumanbey, was hanged three times — once to kill him, twice for good measure — by the Turks in Cairo. The Ottoman Turks installed their own governor, called a pasha, who divided Egypt into 12 provinces and ruled over them all. This government of Turkish pashas lasted about 300 years.

Napoleon

In 1798, the French invaded Egypt to gain control of the land route to the British colony of India. They occupied Alexandria. That year, the anchored fleet under Napoleon Bonaparte, the future emperor of France, was surprised by the attack of British admiral Horatio Nelson. In just two days, Napoleon's forces were annihilated. The French fleet was now stuck in Egypt, though Napoleon himself fled secretly to France, leaving his soldiers behind. The next year, however, Napoleon returned. When Turkish forces in excess of 15,000 men were landed at Alexandria on British ships, Napoleon, with 10,000 men, drove the Turks into the sea, drowning a third of them.

Muhammad Ali

But by 1801, the British and Turks had succeeded in expelling the French. In 1805, after a power struggle, Muhammad Ali, a commander who headed an Albanian Ottoman regiment, seized control. He ruled Egypt for some 40 years. He modernized the country, improving schools and reforming the economic system. He ordered the construction of irrigation and transportation canals, and he introduced cotton cultivation to the Nile Delta.

In his attempt to get rid of all political opponents, Ali carried out a brutal massacre of the remaining Mamelukes in Cairo in 1811. At that time, the Mamelukes were still a powerful force. The new leader invited them to dinner at the Citadel, the great fortress at the center of the city. After dinner, Muhammad Ali waved good-bye to his guests as they made their way down a small, crooked street within the fortress walls. Then the host ordered his soldiers to attack. They killed all the guests save one, who leaped on a horse and tumbled through a gap in a wall and landed in the moat, the water surrounding the Citadel. He survived. Muhammad Ali himself lived until 1849.

Striving for True Representation

During the last half of the 19th century and through the end of World War I, Egyptians hungered for independence. After the death of Muhammad Ali, his descendants ruled Egypt. At the same time, France and Great Britain competed over interests in Egypt.

The French built the great Suez Canal, which opened in 1869, and the Canal fell under British influence in 1876, in large part due to Egyptian mismanagement of money. In that year, France and Britain both agreed to supervise Egypt's messy financial affairs after Ismail, the grandson of Muhammad Ali, had run his country into severe debt.

The British occupied and ruled Egypt in the years to come. Although the British increased public works projects and encouraged political self-expression, Egyptians widely resented their presence. When World War I ended in 1918 and Britain refused to grant independence to Egypt, the Wafd party made its move.

The Wafd party, which had grown into a strong political force during World War I, wanted to end

British rule. It was behind the riots and demonstrations that broke out all over the country in 1919. The British governors restored order, but tensions were high during the years that followed. In 1922, Britain gave Egypt its independence — or nearly did. Egypt became a kingdom, but Britain kept military forces there. The British then ruled behind a series of weak Egyptian kings until 1936, when British troops withdrew from all of Egypt except the Suez Canal area, where they stayed to guard the waterway. The last of the Egyptian kings, Farouk, then took control. He held a grip on the country through World War II. But he feared his end was near as the resistance against him grew even stronger.

The July 1952 Revolution was a momentous event in modern Egyptian history. A group of army officers, led by Gamal Abdel Nasser, forced King Farouk to give up his throne. Egypt now had — for the first time in almost 2,500 years — a government free from outside influence.

Gamal Abdel Nasser

The new president began reforms quickly, at first concentrating on making a more equal distribution of the land. Increased social services, government housing programs, and a new effort at building the public educational system followed.

Nasser was beloved by Egyptians. He could do no wrong. He inspired the people with a new sense of themselves. Pride in their country and culture grew. The Egyptian people supported Nasser despite the war the nation lost to Israel in 1967. Nasser was the focus of Pan-Arabism, the political movement that encouraged unity among the Arab states. It was under his leadership that Egypt joined with Syria to form the United Arab Republic.

Sadat

Upon his death in September 1970, Nasser was succeeded by Anwar el-Sadat. The new president faced many problems. The country was still desperately poor. He made a bold move. Under Nasser, the Soviet Union had been one of Egypt's greatest supporters. But after the Soviets refused to give Sadat additional military aid, he ordered all Soviet advisers to leave Egypt. This allowed Sadat to establish closer ties with the United States. The move pleased Arab conservatives, who were deeply religious Muslims. They disliked communism, because it denies the existence of God.

Sadat proved to be a great world leader. Egypt had been at war with Israel since that nation's birth in 1948, but Sadat flew to Jerusalem in 1977 to make peace with the Israelis. Aided by U.S. president Jimmy Carter, the

President Hosni Mubarak addresses the members of the United Nations.

first peace agreement between an Arab country and Israel was signed in 1979. It was a tremendous and bold move by the Egyptian leader. But there were many in the Arab world who were angry with Sadat for making peace with the Jewish state. One fall day in 1981, Sadat was assassinated while reviewing his troops near Cairo.

With the death of Sadat came the election of his vice president, Hosni Mubarak. A former pilot and deputy minister of war, Mubarak gained a reputation early in life for being a master strategist and a commander who preferred to be among his men at the most critical moments. One of those critical moments appeared in 1990.

The Gulf War

In August of 1990, Saddam Hussein of Iraq invaded Kuwait, claiming it as his own. President Mubarak had to make a difficult decision. He decided to join the multinational effort, led by the United States, against the Iraqi leader. There were several reasons for his decision. Possibly the most important consideration for Mubarak was the offer by the United States to relieve Egypt of its $7 billion American debt. Also, the Egyptian leader was very concerned about the welfare of the more than one million Egyptian workers in Iraq and Kuwait.

   As a result of Egypt's announcement that it was joining the coalition forces, other Arab states got involved in the allied effort, and Hussein's army was crushed and forced to retreat from Kuwait. Mubarak proved himself a decisive leader in world affairs. Egyptians continue to hope that he will lead their nation out of its economic troubles, too.

4. Stories from the Desert

For over 3,000 years, the body of Ramses II lay deep in his tomb in the barren Valley of the Kings, in the desert south of Cairo. Ramses, wrapped in bandages and arms crossed in the traditional manner, is believed by many to have lived at the time of Moses. When discovered and unwrapped just a few years ago, archaeologists watched in amazement as the revealed left hand slowly opened, as if in greeting! Egyptians love this story of their ancient king who communicated to them from the grave!

Ancient Tales

Long adventurous tales, known as romances, were popular in ancient Egypt. These tales were written by priests on papyrus, a paper made from the papyrus plant that still grows today on the banks of the Nile. One such tale, known as "The Story of the Two Brothers," was recently discovered and is thought to have originated in 1250 B.C. New papyrus manuscripts are always being discovered, linking tales from Egypt's past to its present.

The jinn *were supposed to have lived in underground tombs like this one in the Valley of the Kings.*

Jinn

Some of the Egyptians' favorite stories are about the *jinn.* Only 100 years ago, many Arabs still believed in the jinn. Jinn are supernatural beings who are invisible but can assume the shapes of people and beasts. The jinn are said to follow Islam and are also known as *afreet,* or ghouls. Ghouls are supposed to be dead evil beings who rob graves and feed on corpses. The jinn, however, can be good or bad. Many Arabs believed that the jinn erected the pyramids.

Arab legend has it that the jinn were formed from fire before God created Adam and that they dwell between earth and heaven. They eavesdrop on angels and report to earthly magicians or diviners seeking their help. They also live in ancient temples and tombs, feed on the dead, and kill and eat the living. They die only after centuries of life.

Because jinn were thought to assume the forms of animals, like cats and dogs, beating these pets was strongly discouraged for fear that they might in fact be jinn. One tale concerns a conversation between a black cat guarding his master's house and a hungry jinn at the door:

"Open the door," the jinn demanded. The cat looked up and said, "The lock on the door has had the name of God pronounced upon it," explaining why he could not let the evil creature inside. The hungry jinn then asked for two loaves of bread.

Again the cat refused, explaining that the name of God was on all the food in the house, too. When the jinn demanded a jar of water, the cat gave the same reply as before. The jinn was starving now, but the cat refused to let him inside. "Go next door," offered the cat, and the jinn, thwarted, scowled and disappeared.

The next morning the cat's owner heard of his pet's heroic behavior and decided the cat might be a jinn in disguise. The master gave his pet a larger portion of food than usual and then asked it to get him some gold, as jinn are able to do. But the cat was insulted. He turned away and ran off, never to be seen again.

"Nights" at Night

While stories are available in print, Egyptians also enjoy them on radio and television shows. In the early 1950s, many families would settle down in front of the radio every evening at 7:00 P.M. to listen to a 15-minute broadcast of a story from *A Thousand and One Nights*. This is a famous collection of ancient tales, also known as the *Arabian Nights*. They begin with the story of King Shahriyar, who has learned that his wife has been unfaithful. He orders her to be killed and vows to marry a new young maiden every night and have her beheaded the following morning.

One brave and beautiful woman, Scheherazade, determines to be the ruler's next bride. On her wedding night, she tells the king a tale so entertaining that he allows her to live another day to finish it. He allows her to tell another tale, and then another, until she has entertained him for a 1,001 nights. By then, the king has fallen in love with her.

Like King Shahriyar, modern Egyptians listening to the radio had to wait until the following evening to find out how each story ended!

"Ali Baba and the Forty Thieves," one of the more popular stories of the *Arabian Nights,* is still a favored bedtime tale for Egyptian children. The poor woodcutter Ali Baba gains entrance to a secret cave by using the magic words "Open Sesame." After finding a hoard of gold, he is pursued by thieves. With the help of the female slave Morgiana, he kills the thieves by pouring boiling oil over them.

Goha

A distinctly Egyptian story features Goha, who is a poor man living in a village with his son and his donkey. All of the Goha stories, besides being amusing, have a moral. Here is one story:

As they were passing through a town, Goha's son became tired, so he rode on the donkey. People cursed them and called the son disrespectful for not letting the father ride the donkey.

Goha himself climbed onto the donkey. But people started to call him lazy. Goha and his son looked at

At home in the evening, an Egyptian mother tells her daughter a story while they play.

each other, then picked up the donkey and carried it between them. Now everybody called them stupid! The moral? People are constantly judging you no matter what you do!

The Evil Eye

This is the superstition that the envious glance of any passerby could harm or bewitch a person showing off his or her own wealth or beauty. To ward off the evil eye, a person can recite certain verses of the Koran. Also, a bracelet with the representation of the *Uzait Horun,* or Eye of Horus (an ancient Egyptian god), can be worn. In Egypt today you will see a single eye painted on cars, trucks, and fishing boats. This is supposed to repel the evil eye. Also, children leave their handprints on walls to distract the evil eye.

Some people now think that the belief in the evil eye may have helped Egyptians feel more or less equal to one another, in terms of wealth. While a poor Egyptian couldn't afford the land and property of a rich neighbor, he had the power to put a curse on him!

Jokes

Jokes are very popular in Egypt. Egyptians tell jokes to release the tensions and frustrations of daily life, which are many! They believe they could not live without jokes, and they try to take the worst things in their daily lives and make jokes about them.

Egyptians have a joke about shortages and waiting in lines. There are often severe shortages of goods — like food and other necessities — and people have to wait in long lines just for the chance to buy them. Sometimes the lines are so long that when people see one, they just get on it. They think that so many people in a line must mean that something very desirable is being offered for sale. After they get in line, they ask somebody what they're waiting to buy.

A joke about lines is as follows: A man was walking along the street, suddenly put his hand to his forehead, and went to the door of a store getting ready to open. Someone went to stand behind him, then another, and within a few minutes there was a line down the block. A man came along and was curious about what the line was for. He went to the last person and asked, but that person didn't know. The person ahead of him didn't know either. The man asked and asked and finally came to the first person.

"What are they selling?" he asked.

The first man looked up with pain on his face. "I don't know. I just had a headache."

Egyptians also like to make jokes about their bureaucracy. In Egypt, each person with a government job has a very narrow responsibility, as though each works in a factory and is responsible for doing only one specialized thing, such as turning a screw or tightening a lid on a jar. The bureaucrats are thought by most Egyptians to blindly follow orders, without using their own

judgment. As a result, it takes a long time to get any-
thing done, because every action has to be approved by
a lot of people and meet fixed rules. Getting a simple
official document can take months.

One joke about the Egyptian bureaucracy goes like
this: A fox was escaping from Egypt when he met a
camel on his way into Egypt. The fox stopped the camel
and warned him, "Don't go to Egypt! They get a hold of
camels and work them to death!"

The camel was upset upon hearing this. "But why
are you running away?" he asked the fox. "You are not a
camel."

The fox shrugged and replied, "You know it and I
know it. But I would have a very difficult time produc-
ing the papers to prove it!"

5. *Egyptian Celebrations*

In ancient times, Egyptians honored the springtime. When the Nile's waters reached a certain height, a young girl would be sacrificed to the river god. This was supposed to ensure a good flood. In modern times, a straw image of a girl, called *el-arusa,* or bride of the Nile, is sent into the river from a decorated boat off Roda Island, in Cairo. Even though the High Dam at Aswan has stopped the floods and provided a regular flow of water, the Egyptians still make this symbolic gesture every spring.

Shem al-Nessim

Egyptians celebrate the advent of springtime with the holiday called *Shem al-Nessim*. This is a national holiday, which falls on the first Monday after the Coptic celebration of Easter. On this day, the entire population, no matter what religion, takes a day off from work or school. Shem al-Nessim means "scent of the breeze," which is what Egyptians get at this wonderfully hopeful time of year, when Nile River plants and flowers begin to grow and bloom. The ancient Egyptians believed that on this spring day the earth was born.

When Shem al-Nessim comes, everybody wants to be outside to celebrate. People in the cities go to the parks or, if they are able, drive into the countryside. Children dress in colorful clothes and enjoy picnics with their parents.

This is a special day for children who live in villages, too. They go out into their fields or gardens to eat and play games. They help their parents decorate feluccas with garlands of flowers, and they all go for rides up and down the Nile.

On Shem al-Nessim, Egyptians eat a special breakfast of fisikh — a salted fish — fresh onions, beans, and hard-boiled eggs. Like American children at Eastertime, Egyptian children like to decorate eggs and eat them, too. The fish and onions are said to prevent disease, while the eggs symbolize life.

Maulid al-Nabi

Maulid al-Nabi is a national feast day, held on the birthday of the prophet Muhammad. Days before, people are busy with preparations. Decorations are made and special foods are cooked. Children enjoy making little brightly colored paper dresses that they put on sweet cookies shaped like dolls. These are a special feast-day dessert. On the holiday, people go to mosques to hear special prayers and stories recited and music performed.

At night, all the mosques, with their broad domes and slender minarets, are lit up in celebration.

Villagers in the western oasis of Siwa, not far from the Libyan border, have developed interesting customs associated with this holiday. The women as a group prepare a special dish called belila, which is a mixture of rice, water, beans, corn, and wheat. They bring the dish with them as they visit friends and relatives in nearby towns. As part of the day's celebrations, they trade tastes of their dish for food from other towns.

Ramadan

Ramadan is a month of fasting from dawn to sunset each day. It begins with the sighting of the new moon on the first day of the ninth month of the Muslim year. During Ramadan, adults fast so that they can understand what it is like to be poor and hungry. It takes great discipline to go a full day without tasting a drop of water or bite of food! Children under 12 are only allowed to fast once or twice a week, and then for just a few hours. Elderly people do not have to fast at all.

Each day before the sun comes up, adults have a light meal. Then the fast begins. Working hours are usually cut short to reduce afternoon effort to a minimum. Nothing is permitted to pass the lips during fasting hours, though non-Muslim visitors are allowed to eat, drink, and smoke.

(Previous pages) An oasis in bloom during Shem al-Nessim, *the festival of spring.*

At sunset, the cannon shot from the Citadel and the call from the minarets signal the start of the evening meal, or *iftar*. This is the meal everyone loves, especially children. Besides enjoying a delicious dinner with their parents, they are encouraged to go from house to house swinging colored lanterns and singing Ramadan songs.

Eid al-Fitr

At the end of Ramadan, there are three days of feasting and celebration, called *Eid al-Fitr.* On the last day of Ramadan, when the new moon is in the sky, everyone waits eagerly for the *feteer,* or breaking of the fast. The moment the sun sets, Eid al-Fitr begins. This end of the fast is announced by the happy beating of drums all over the country.

Eid means "feast," and there is a great feast for the whole family. Cookies and other sweets are baked and given out after the feast, with special sweet cakes called *kahk.*

There is gift-giving during Eid al-Fitr, too. Children usually get new clothes from their parents for the Eid celebration, and they receive gifts of money from their uncles and aunts and grandparents so that they can buy what they want. Family celebrations like this are among the best parts of the year for Muslim children.

In a cafe in Cairo, Egyptians celebrate the end of Ramadan to the sound of drum and pipe.

Eid al-Adha comes later in the year. This is the time for Muslims to fulfill one of the commands of Islam — the pilgrimage to Mecca. Every Muslim must try to make the journey at least once. Eid al-Adha also commemorates a story in the Koran that is taken from the Old Testament. In it, God tests the faith of Ibrahim (Abraham) when he asks him to sacrifice his son Ismail (Isaac). Satisfied that Ibrahim is willing to kill his son, God provides a ram for him to sacrifice instead. On this important holiday, Egyptians slaughter a lamb, symbolic of the ram. They eat it with rice as part of a formal dinner.

Other Holidays

Though not in the Muslim calendar, many Egyptians like to celebrate Christmas Eve and New Year's Eve. Christmas Eve parties are popular with Egypt's Christians, the Copts, and with less-religious Muslims, who live mostly in the large cities. These gatherings are quieter and not so well attended as the New Year's Eve parties to come. Usually, friends meet at a private club or at somebody's home.

On New Year's Eve, many Egyptians like to attend lively parties and listen to Western music. But New Year's Day is not a holiday, and everybody has to get up the next morning to go to work or school.

The Christian feast of the Epiphany is also celebrated in Egypt. Historically, January 6 was also the day that the water of the Nile was supposed to be at its purest. The early Copts would collect Nile water in sacred containers and save it, to be used during special holy events throughout the year. This ritual is still followed by modern-day Copts, who draw the Nile water for the coming year's baptisms and sacraments.

The Seven-Day Party

The Seven-Day Party is not an official holiday. It celebrates a birth in a family. Each person who comes to the house (mostly relatives of the newborn's parents) is received with kisses and is given individual attention. Everyone is drawn into conversation, and no one is left out, especially the newborn, whose demands are attended to by everyone.

During the Seven-Day Party, every guest has a place and is essential to the well-being of the entire group. People participate in this party by conversing or by serving others. The mood is always kept relaxed and friendly. For instance, when elders talk during the Seven-Day Party, children are encouraged not to leave the room — they are to feel valued as equals at this special time. They are shown that togetherness and sociability are important values — in each family, and among all Egyptians.

6. *Family and Food in Egypt*

In Egypt, the family unit is very strong. In most house-holds, single men and women live with their families until they marry. Also, mothers who work outside the home leave their children with relatives during the day. This can make for a busy day in a crowded house! But as the day winds down and evening approaches, the attitude is relaxed — "we'll get to it tomorrow." Egyptians don't like to rush through life — they'd rather linger and enjoy themselves, especially when they are with their families at home.

Mud, Concrete, and Tombs

Homes in Egypt range from the mud-and-straw houses of villagers to the massive concrete-block apartment buildings crowding the big cities. You can find people living in the ancient tombs of the City of the Dead in Cairo or in Alexandria's lovely old apartment buildings with ornate grillwork balconies. These houses are a reminder of the French presence in Egypt.

In the villages, houses are fairly similar to one

another. They are made of mud bricks and wood from palm trees, and they look like the adobe houses found in the United States' Southwest. They have small windows shuttered against the sun and are usually clustered around the village square and the well (*bir*) at its center.

The roofs of village houses serve many purposes. They are always flat, for storing food, firewood, and fertilizer. Also, dates and other foods can be laid out to dry on large trays made of palm leaves. Granaries made of mud are sometimes kept on the roof, storing and protecting grains and other foods from birds and animals. Dovecotes, or homes for doves and other birds, are also kept on the roof. And clotheslines are strung along the roof so that wet clothes are fully exposed to the hot sun.

The sun is merciless, and a village home owner is fortunate if he can build his house beneath the sheltering leaves of a date-palm tree. Date palms are valuable trees to the Egyptian villagers. Besides providing delicious fruit, they serve several functions. The leaves are woven into mats and baskets. The stems of the leaves are whittled down and gathered into useful brooms.

In the cities, many Egyptians live in apartment buildings. While some are old and charming, their designs influenced by the British and French, most are made of harsh-looking concrete blocks. These are huge buildings, with many families living in rows of standardized apartments.

Sharing and Caring

Whether living in houses or apartments, children in a family almost always share rooms. They are not encouraged to have a strong sense of individual property. Instead, clothing, toys, and appliances are shared.

Cars are shared among family members, too, though most people prefer to travel by public transportation. The subway and buses are crowded and not always reliable, but they're safer than cars. Egyptians are not terribly concerned about following traffic rules! Also, gas and auto repairs are expensive, and many youngsters simply cannot afford their own cars. But they can manage without them. In the cities the streets are crowded and parking is hard to find, and in the villages everything can be reached by foot or donkey. When you can ride a bicycle or even a donkey to work or to school, who needs a car?

Pets are always shared among children in a family. Youngsters especially favor goats as pets. Cows and lambs, though not considered pets, are prized possessions. But since there is usually little land for them, they sometimes sleep in the house with the family. They are generally treated as well as pets.

After children do homework and chores, they can go play with their friends. However, unlike American children, when Egyptian boys and girls visit the houses of their friends, they bring along their brothers or sisters.

A crowded street in Cairo — it would be difficult to park a car here!

It doesn't matter if they are much younger or of the other sex. In Egypt, emphasis is placed on family activities. When children reach age 17 or so, though, they are basically on their own when they visit one another or go to parties.

If there's nothing to do, kids can always stay home and watch television together. Egyptian soap operas are popular during the day, and Egyptian comedy shows are fun to watch at night. But Egyptians also like to watch reruns of "Dallas" and "Knot's Landing" — in Arabic, of course!

Dating and Marriage

In Egypt, dating is taken very seriously. Since boys and girls always attend separate high schools, young people have few ways to meet except through introductions by family members. Even if a boy and girl meet on their own, they must inform their parents and get permission to continue seeing each other. Egyptian families view dating as a direct preparation for marriage.

In villages, marriages are often arranged. A woman must wait until a young man or his family shows interest in her. Then, however, she can accept or reject her suitor. In urban areas, people can meet in clubs, at work, or through friends. After meeting, they will get to know each other. If they are compatible, the man talks to the

Men heed the calls of the muezzin *from a Cairo minaret.*

woman's parents. If that goes well, and all parties are agreeable, the couple gets engaged and throws a party, either for just the immediate family or for 200 to 300 people!

The couple remains engaged for a while, then they get married in a religious ceremony. Rings are exchanged, and the bride's parents give a dowry, or a sum of money, to the groom. Traditionally, the bride's parents also buy furniture, and the groom's parents buy the apartment and car — though today it's not always easy to afford this! Finally, the happy couple go on their honeymoon. If they have the money, they fly to the Red Sea or Aswan or sail on a Nile cruise, or even go off to Europe. They always leave the wedding reception in a car decorated with flowers and with the horn honking!

The Role of Women

Called the "Daughters of the Nile," Egyptian women were once considered to be the mere property of their husbands. While they were still young girls, their families selected future husbands for them. Until recently, most Westerners thought that Egyptian women found jobs only in nightclubs, as belly dancers, and there was some truth in this thinking. But life has changed for women in Egypt, especially for those who live in the cities.

In modern Egypt, women not only dance in nightclubs but also manage and own them. They run clothing stores and restaurants. Women in Egypt are mayors, pilots, ship captains, and bank directors. Currently, about half of all the nation's medical graduates are women.

Even the women in the smallest and most conservative villages have a kind of independence. It has been forced on them by poverty. Lacking jobs at home, the village men have had to leave to find work in other Arab countries. So many men have been forced to leave, in fact, that some villages in the Nile Delta and in Upper Egypt now have no adult males at all! That leaves the women to do the men's jobs — planting crops, buying and selling livestock, and making important decisions for the family.

Hospitality

The ancient Egyptians enjoyed the pleasures of life. They liked to dress up and wear jewelry and put makeup on their faces, and they especially liked to get together for grand feasts. They held festive banquets with many varieties of food to eat. They were entertained by singers and dancers. Guests liked to make many toasts to friendship.

Sharing and hospitality are values encouraged in every modern Egyptian family. When children have sweets, they are encouraged to give some to others before taking any for themselves. The smallest children are usually given the job of handing out sweets to guests at parties, so that they can learn and practice these important values. *Min fadlak* (please), says the child, holding out a tray of sweets. *Shukran* (thank you), says the guest, and the child bows and goes on to the next adult.

Food

Bread, or *aish*, is the basic food of the Egyptian people. A flat, dishlike loaf is given to each family member with every meal. In a family, each person might eat up to a pound of bread per day! Other basic foods are sugar — for tea and coffee — cooking oil, beans, and vegetables.

The fellahin make a round, flat bread called *balady*, which they fill with various mixtures. The bread is flat because there is no yeast in it. At lunch, they might fill the bread with goat cheese and onions, and in the evening they may stuff it with beans or lentils.

Instead of buying bread, many families make it themselves. A woman takes grains of corn or wheat and roasts them in an oven, which is made of clay. After roasting, the grains are placed in a bowl and pounded into flour. Dough is made by adding water to the flour, and this is spread out on a wooden board and put into the oven. In two minutes the dough is transformed into a flat loaf of bread, fresh and hot.

The fellahin often cook other foods over a charcoal fire. They don't have timber or coal to burn. A large copper bowl — sometimes even an old gasoline can — serves as the pot.

Though supermarkets are becoming popular, Egyptians generally like to buy their food fresh. They do not like to buy meat that has been sitting in a refrigerator for several days. So they shop at stores that specialize in

A brass merchant's stall in the Khan El-Khalili bazaar.
The markets are busy at all hours of the day in Cairo.

one category of food like the butcher shop and the vegetable market.

Meals

For breakfast people usually have beans and milk, then rush out to their jobs. They often buy more food on the way to work. They will stop at a food stall in the village square for baked bread wrapped around fried eggplants, beans, tomatoes, and peppers. Even in the cities, people buy from the food stalls.

At lunch, workers take time out for meat on skewers. Kabab, which is the dish that is most popular, consists of pieces of lamb or beef marinated in a mixture of lemon juice, olive oil, sliced onions, pepper, and salt, and then grilled over coals. It is available on many Cairo street corners. Tahini is often served with it. This creamy white sauce is a paste of sesame seeds to which oil and garlic have been added.

Ful is a popular Egyptian dish and is often eaten for dinner. It consists of cooked fava beans mixed with hot peppers, garlic, and oil, and is served with a variety of foods. These broad beans are also used to make soups and stews. Cucumbers and dates are eaten with the evening meal. Roast pigeon is a favorite Egyptian dish. It is usually split down the middle and then grilled over charcoal.

Tea is the most popular drink. Tea leaves are added

to water and the water is boiled. Sugar is poured into the pot, and the tea is served sweet and strong.

A dinner ends with desserts. Fresh fruit is popular, as are sweet little cakes. Children like to drink laban, which is a creamy drink made from goat's yogurt diluted with water and flavored with salt. Children also drink a mixture of tea and sherbet, which is very sweet.

One favorite dessert is *mahallabiya,* a mixture of rice, milk, rose water, sugar, and nuts. It melts in your mouth. *Aish al-Seraya* is popular, too. It is simply honey and butter heated and combined with breadcrumbs. When it is cool, thick cream from the top of cooked milk can be skimmed off and spread on top like icing. Another popular dessert is *bassbusa.* Try making it for your family one night. Remember to have a parent help you.

Bassbusa

3 cups sugar
2 cups plain yogurt
2 cups uncooked semolina (or Cream of Wheat)
1 tablespoon baking soda

Syrup:

1 1/2 cups sugar
1 1/2 cups water
(Boil sugar and water 5 minutes and add several drops of lemon juice.)

☛Mix the sugar, yogurt, semolina, and baking soda together and place in a medium-size baking dish in a 350°F (175°C) oven. ☛Bake until brown, about 10 minutes, and then remove. ☛Pour the prepared syrup over the golden bassbusa and slice into squares. ☛Return the baking dish to the oven for a few minutes until the syrup is baked on.

Aish al-Seraya (Palace Bread)

8 oz. honey
4 oz. (one stick) butter
4 oz. white breadcrumbs

☛Heat honey and butter in a saucepan until mixture thickens. Add breadcrumbs. ☛Cook for about 15 minutes, stirring frequently. ☛Scrape mixture onto a plate. ☛When it cools, it will be like a small cake. ☛Cut into triangles and top with whipped cream if you like. ☛Enjoy!

7. A Strained System

Egypt is the center of learning among the Arab states. Many of the colleges and universities in the Arab world are located here. Today there are more than five million graduates from these schools of higher learning. However, the school system in Egypt is under a great strain.

Too Many People!

Overpopulation and limited resources are the causes of the problem. To get an idea of how the system has had to expand, look at the elementary-school population. In 1920, the total number of children in elementary school was 290,000. Just 60 years later, in 1983, that number had increased more than 24 times, to about seven million! In addition, almost 20 million Egyptians—nearly 40 percent of the population—are under the age of 15. Egypt cannot build schools fast enough for its children, but they all need to be educated.

Many families are so poor that they can't afford to have a child in school. The children are needed to work with the parents during the day. The schools try to arrange special evening classes for these children.

But many children don't attend school at all. Only

72 percent of the children who should attend elementary school do so, while in high school the figure is much lower—only 46 percent attend. More urban children—about 90 percent—go to school than children from rural areas. The children from the villages have to help out more on the farms.

For those children who do make it to the classroom,

Once only boys attended school in Egypt. Today, girls and boys are treated as equals.

conditions have been improved to help them learn. School laws enacted in 1972 limit each class to 40 students or less. These laws affected teachers also — they were no longer allowed to knit or eat during classes! Also, pupils were scheduled to be examined at the end of each year, instead of at the end of six years. By the mid-1970s, one-quarter of Egypt's annual budget was being spent each year on education. But even with these improvements, it was not unusual to find, among poor pupils, those who could not read and write even after six years of elementary education.

Suzanne Mubarak, the president's wife, is trying to make the Egyptian school system better. She is chairwoman of the Integrated Care Society for Primary School Children, an organization devoted mainly to establishing libraries in schools. It has set up 30 children's libraries in elementary schools in Cairo and Alexandria as well as 10 children's public libraries in low-income communities. It has also expanded its activities to provide music-listening rooms, to organize recreational and cultural trips for kids, and to aid the school health clinics. The society started its activities in 1977 with one school in western Cairo. Now it is active in over 17 schools teaching more than 22,000 pupils throughout Cairo, with branches in other areas of Egypt as well.

Yesterday and Today

Once, the only schools were religious schools. Boys in a city or village would attend a *kuttab,* or religious school, run by the great Al-Azhar University in Cairo. Often, the kuttab would be in a mosque.

At the kuttab, students would memorize passages of the Koran and talk about Islamic law and the study of Arabic. Boys might begin studying as early as age four and stay for six or seven years. However, few girls were allowed to go to these schools. They had to stay home and help their mothers cook and raise the other children. This would make the girls attractive to potential husbands.

Girls and boys are treated as equals in Egypt's modern school system. All boys and girls ages six to twelve are required to attend school. After these six years of primary school, they must pass an exam to go on to three years of intermediary school. They must pass another exam to be enrolled for three years of secondary or trade school, for a total of twelve years. Education in Egypt is free through the university level, and competition is fierce for admittance to some schools.

Language Schools

Many children attend private schools, also called language schools. The language schools charge tuition and compete for students with the public elementary, intermediate, and secondary schools. About 25 percent of students nationwide are enrolled in the language schools.

One advantage of a language school is that it will teach science and math in a language other than Arabic. The public schools teach all subjects in Arabic. By attending a language school, a student becomes better prepared for working outside of Egypt after graduation. On the other hand, some say that the language schools are

A school in a small village. Unfortunately, many children in Egypt don't get the chance to attend school at all.

less competitive than the public schools because students with poor grades can buy their way into them. Luckily, families don't have to decide between language and public schools until the children are out of primary school.

The School Day

Primary-school education is standard throughout Egypt. The youngest children start school at 7:00 A.M. This is the morning session. An afternoon session starts at 1:00 P.M. and uses the same room. The boys and girls attend school together, with six years of learning side-by-side. Then they go to separate intermediary schools.

In primary school, all of the children wear uniforms. Beige and navy blue are popular colors for most schools, though boys might wear gray pants and shirt and a burgundy sweater in the winter. Every school also has its own badge, which is sewn onto their uniforms.

There used to be stricter guidelines for dressing. Every child had to wear white socks and polished black shoes. The uniform had to be cleaned and ironed every day. Wearing makeup was forbidden, as were any kind of fancy hairstyles. Teachers began the day with a morning inspection, and each child had to present his or her fingernails to show that they were clean. Today, the schools are not as strict. Uniforms, though, are still mandatory.

Much of the day in primary school is spent learning Arabic. The Arabic alphabet has 28 letters, and Arabic words are written from right to left. Sentence structure and grammar resemble that of Hebrew, its sister language. As with Hebrew, vowels in Arabic are not part of the alphabet and are written above the word. Arabic is one of the most widely spoken languages in the world — well over 100 million people speak it — and all students know how important it is to read and write it correctly. They use Arabic to learn other subjects, such as science, math, and history.

There is much to study in school, but time is always taken for breaks, too. Children have snacks and exercise breaks at midmorning and in the afternoon, and sometimes they go on class trips. They like to go to the Cairo Zoo and the Egyptian Museum. Another favorite spot is the new Natural History Museum for Children in Cairo. Similar to natural history museums in the United States, it tries to develop an understanding and love of nature in the children, as well as a desire to protect the environment. Teachers also try to instill these values in their students.

Teachers hold a high place in Egyptian society. People look up to them. They are hired after receiving an extensive education from one of the country's 32 teachers' colleges. Most schoolteachers in Egypt today are women; many of the male teachers in recent years have been lured to oil-rich Arab countries.

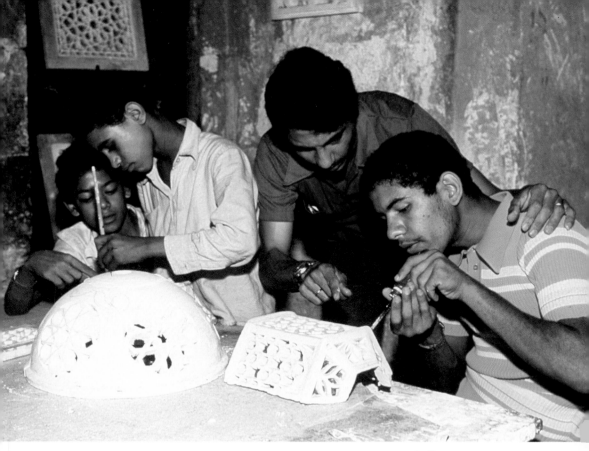

Students taking a technical course learn important skills.

Male or female, a teacher must help the students do well in primary school. At the completion of the mandatory six years, the student is given a Primary Certificate Examination. This is a hard test and must be passed if the student is to be admitted to the intermediate schools. At the end of intermediate school, which lasts three years (like our junior high schools), the student must take another exam. If this is passed, the student is admitted to high school. But the tests are hard, and so, too, is life outside of school for the Egyptian children. It is estimated that nine out of ten children beginning primary school do not graduate from high school.

High School

After completing primary school, students have to decide whether to attend a private or public school. In both intermediate and secondary school, students may choose between academic or technical courses of study. In technical schools they learn specific skills to get them jobs when they graduate.

A typical day at a public school includes English and French lessons. English is begun in seventh grade, while students learn French in the eleventh grade. Students who have time and ability participate in sports. Every school has several athletic teams and coaches.

After school, students go home and do their homework. However, studying is often difficult due to crowded conditions. A student may have to do his or her homework at the kitchen table where the mother is preparing dinner and the baby is crying.

Because students have rigorous final exams, which they must pass to be admitted to the next grade, they often get help from tutors. Math and science teachers especially make large amounts of money tutoring students, mostly at the secondary level. This can make education costly, and difficult for most families to afford.

Finally, after school and their tutoring session, the children can go outside to play. Then they think about vacation! They have one week's vacation in January and four months off in the summer.

Higher Education

Admission to the universities is based on a student's marks on a special secondary school examination. This exam is very difficult, and getting accepted to college is a great achievement in the life of an Egyptian student. Egypt has 13 universities, and more than 40,000 students graduate from them each year.

Al-Azhar is Cairo's religious university. Built in A.D. 971, it is the oldest university in the world. Today, it is among the most highly respected Islamic universities in the world. It is also considered one of the best examples of Islamic architecture.

From *kuttab* to coed, Egypt has come a long way from its traditional educational system. Once, the kuttabs were the only schools, and girls were discouraged from even entering them. Today, at Al-Azhar University, Islam's most prestigious school, there are 18,000 students — of which 8,000 are women.

8. *From Soccer to Scuba Diving*

Though a desert nation, Egypt has a great many sporting activities. "Egypt offers everything but ice skating," says Abdulaleem el-Abyad of the Egyptian Mission to the United Nations in New York.

At an early age, Egyptian children play games such as hopscotch, jump rope (girls only), marbles, and table tennis. When they are older, children are introduced to organized sports at school. There they learn gymnastics, volleyball, basketball, swimming, and tennis.

Every school has coaches and teams for the various sports. Government youth centers feature organized activities for the poor children in the cities and villages. Students from more prosperous families can join teams at private sports clubs.

Sports Clubs

Sports clubs are similar to American country clubs. They offer sports facilities, restaurants, and cafes, all suited for family use. The clubs are private and one becomes a member only upon recommendation by another member. There are seven major sports clubs in

Egyptian students are offered many kinds of sporting activities at school. Here, children participate in gymnastics.

Cairo, including the National, Zamalek, Al-Ahli, Ismaili, Masri, Heliopolis, and Champs. There are also about 20 other smaller ones that might not have soccer fields. There is a huge club in Alexandria and moderate-size clubs in other major cities.

The Egyptian sports clubs are much more complete than American country clubs. A large club—set on a huge, fenced-in plot of land—may have a soccer stadium seating 20,000 to 30,000 fans! It may offer 25 tennis courts, 10 basketball courts, 10 volleyball courts, and an Olympic-size swimming pool with a kiddie pool!

Some clubs also offer croquet, miniature golf, table tennis, and horseback riding. All have a main building with halls for parties, movie theaters, and cafeterias. These clubs have everything! After a long, hard day of playing soccer, a tired member can even meet with friends after dark for an outdoor movie at the club.

Soccer

When it comes to sports in Egypt, first there is soccer, then there is everything else. You can find soccer (which the Egyptians and most of the world call football) being played everywhere — in the streets, in the clubs, in any empty space. Children grow up kicking balls — or cans, bottles, or rocks — in the streets. Everyone plays soccer in Egypt!

Soccer is even played inside apartments. In the cities, kids who live in large apartment complexes sometimes don't want to go down to the street or to a club, or maybe it's just too hot to go out. Then they play with a *sharab,* a homemade ball. A sharab, which is Arabic for "socks," is an old sponge with socks wrapped around it. Ideally, it's the size of a cantaloupe. Many famous players started out playing with sharabs. Parents are used to seeing sharabs sailing around the apartment!

When they play soccer in the street, the children have to decide on goals. During official games at school, the goals are made of upright supports with a net fastened to them. In the street, though, Egyptian children do what American children do: They use shirts or coats as boundaries and they agree on a kick after it's performed. "It's too high," one side yells. "It's not too high!" yells the other side. After a little arguing, they come to a decision.

World Competition

Egypt has long been competitive on the world soccer stage. In the 1930s, the National team came very close to winning the world championship. Egypt was also the first Arab and African state to take part in the World Cup selections in Italy in 1934. Its team won the African Cup in 1957, 1958, and 1986. It also won the esteemed Cup of the Champion Clubs in 1982 and 1983.

Among the sports-club teams, Atelie and Zamalek are the two most popular in Cairo. They have the most fans. Egyptian soccer fans are enthusiastic but not rowdy like the fans of European teams. One reason for this may be that alcohol is not sold at the stadiums. Juices and soft drinks are consumed in great quantities, though, because of the hot, dry climate.

The largest soccer stadium in Egypt is Cairo Sta-

Soccer is Egypt's favorite sport. Here, two professional players pose for the camera.

dium. It is located in downtown Cairo, next to the Anwar Sadat Memorial, where the former leader is buried. The stadium seats 100,000 and is part of a big complex where many sports are played. However, important soccer games are also played at the stadium of the National Club, one of the larger sports clubs in Cairo.

Girls are not encouraged to play soccer. Why not? One Egyptian man thinks that there is "too much contact and the movements too vigorous for the woman's physique. It's dangerous for them, like boxing." Many girls don't agree, however, and they "break the rules" by playing soccer with their friends!

Swimming and Rowing

In the 1950s and 1960s, many world-class long-distance swimmers were from Egypt. Swimming is popular among all classes of society, and people admire athletes like Abdel-Baqui Hassanein, the first Arab to cross the English Channel. Many children look up to the handicapped swimmer Khaled Hassan, who inspired other handicapped Egyptians to participate in sports.

Egypt's champion swimmers used to train by swimming up the Nile. People in Cairo would take a break from work or school and go down to the river to watch. But training in the Nile stopped in the 1960s, when pollution became too great. However, swimmers have been training for many years in the Suez Canal, and still do. There they enjoy racing the international shipping traffic!

The rowing clubs practice on the Nile River. There are about ten independent rowing clubs in Egypt. You can go down to the water and watch the Police Club, the Military Club, and clubs from the many universities practicing or competing with one another in their long boats. Sometimes teams from other countries are invited to compete. The boats glide smoothly by the barges, feluccas, and the other slow-moving water traffic of the Nile.

Sports Heroes

Soccer star Saleh Salem played on the National team in the 1960s. He also played on foreign teams, as did the great Magdy Abdul-Gany, who played at one time for Portuguese teams. Ahmed Sho'eir, the goalkeeper on the National team, trained at the National Sports Club. His teammate on the National team for years has been Gala Abd-El Hamid, chosen best player in Egypt in 1987. He's been a member of the National team since he was 20 years old, and is admired by fans for his discipline and sporting spirit.

The most famous Egyptian tennis star was Smail al-Shafee. He competed at Wimbledon for many years until the 1970s. And judo champion Mohamed Ali Rashwan is a national figure, too. Born in Alexandria,

A rowing team swiftly approaches a felucca on the Nile.

he won the bronze medal in the U.S. Military World Championship in 1981 and 1982. In 1983, he won fifth place in the world competition in Moscow.

Water Sports

Because the beaches at Port Said and Alexandria are often crowded, many Egyptians flock to the Red Sea. Tourist villages have sprung up at Red Sea resorts and are very popular with foreigners. Middle-class Egyptians also like to get away from Cairo and other hot cities and come to the clean waters for a vacation. While Egyptian women dress conservatively in their towns and cities, here they are free to wear bikinis like the Western tourists.

Scuba diving is becoming more and more popular among Egyptians. Resorts on the Red Sea, such as Sharm el-Sheikh, Nuweiba, and Dahab in the southern Sinai, are popular spots for this sport. The diving season is year-round, with water temperatures ranging from 70°F (21°C) in winter to 80°F (27°C) in summer.

Scuba diving in the Red Sea can be fascinating: You can see colorful coral and many varieties of fish, including clownfish, angelfish, wrasse, rays, and even barracudas and sharks. Some can be fed from your hand, but others, like scorpion fish, are poisonous and must be avoided!

Egyptians admire excellence in swimming. This enormous pool is part of a private sports club in Cairo.

Egyptians also like to spend time in another kind of water: mineral springs. They believe that these springs heal the body of its ailments. There are different springs in different parts of the country for different ailments. Ein al-Sira, just south of Cairo, offers waters that heal rheumatism. And the sulfur-enriched waters at the Siwa Oasis in the Western Desert help in the treatment of skin diseases. Helwan, nearly 30 miles (48 kilometers) south of Cairo, is known as the City of Health and offers numerous springs for the weary visitor. Even if one does not have a specific ailment, these natural springs are delightful and relaxing.

Finally, Egyptians have a new water park to look forward to. Planned for a barren desert hillside about 45 minutes from downtown Cairo, the new American-style park will have plenty of water. It will have water slides, chutes, and inner-tube rides. In fact, water will have to be trucked in from the Nile River at the rate of 45,000 gallons every three days! "Just like California," insists the excited Egyptian developer.

9. *Far from the Nile*

While Egyptians have always had great pride in their country, in recent years many of them have had to travel to other nations to find work. About ten years ago, Egyptians began to emigrate to the oil-rich countries of the Persian Gulf — nations such as Saudi Arabia, Bahrain, and Kuwait. In need of unskilled workers, these countries have welcomed the arriving Egyptians as well as nationals from many other third-world countries. Foreign workers in the Gulf states earn good salaries and send them to their wives and children back home.

The Flight to America

Egyptians began emigrating to the United States back in the early 1950s. After Nasser came to power in 1952, he nationalized, or brought under government control, many banks and businesses that had been privately owned. As a result of this and other reforms, the poor began to be treated better by the government — but the wealthier Egyptians had to give up some of what they had. Some of the wealthy Egyptians were able to move to the United States. But U.S. immigration quotas, or limits, prevented others from settling there.

An Egyptian American stops to read an Arabic-language newspaper in a store in Brooklyn, New York.

In 1968, the American quotas were eased, and many Egyptians began to emigrate to the United States. In the two years after the quota change, almost 50,000 Egyptians came to the United States. Today, there are approximately 150,000 to 200,000 Egyptians living in the United States.

The majority of Egyptian Americans are from the educated class and have college degrees. They are professionals or entrepreneurs (people who start and run their own businesses). You will not find many fellahin among Egyptian Americans. Egyptian farmers are tied to their land and generally do not emigrate.

Many Egyptians in the United States have settled in communities with other Arabs, like the Syrians and Lebanese. There are large communities of Egyptians in Los Angeles and nearby Orange County, as well as in Jersey City, New Jersey, and Brooklyn, New York.

Naturally, most of the new immigrants feel more at home in communities where Arabic is spoken. But many Egyptians do not hesitate to mix with Americans. All, however, experience difficult adjustments to life in the West.

A Period of Adjustment

When Egyptians first come to the United States, they suffer from loneliness, like other immigrants. They miss their friends and the social life back home. Television and radio programs are not understood because of the language barrier. Everything is so new and different!

Gradually, they begin to understand American ways

a little. Often, they don't approve of all of them. Egyptian immigrants are not used to the informal way Americans address one another. They especially object to the way children speak to their elders. Back home, elders are always held in reverence — so much so that Egyptian children regard their parents as "holy figures." American children, say these immigrants, don't exhibit the proper *ehtran,* or respect.

Egyptians are not very pleased with the way Americans dress, either. Egyptians take pride in dressing as well as they can afford to. They find it troubling to see Americans wearing torn jeans and T-shirts in public!

Egyptian Americans

Before most Egyptians arrive in the United States, they have an idea of the sights and rhythms of American life. An Egyptian engineer described his first few days in New York: "Like all over the world, American movies are there [in Egypt], and you get an idea what America is from the movies. When I got to Rockefeller Center, it was like coming to a place I already knew. Park Avenue and Grand Central Station and the crowds coming and going in and out at 5:00 P.M. — these are the images I had in my mind. I knew what New Orleans would be like from watching *Cat on a Hot Tin Roof.*"

Some Egyptians have found success in the Ameri-

A Middle Eastern grocery store in Brooklyn, New York. Egyptian Americans like to cook the same dishes they enjoyed back home.

can entertainment industry, like Omar Sharif. Born Michel Shalhoub in Alexandria in 1932, he moved to Cairo with his family at age four and as a teenager joined the drama groups at Victoria College. After appearing in 24 Egyptian films and two French productions, he played in *Lawrence of Arabia,* a film that brought him worldwide attention. After this he did most of his work with Columbia Pictures in Hollywood. His greatest success was in the lead role in the film *Doctor Zhivago.*

Assad Kelada, a former Cairene, is the producer of two hit television shows, *Who's the Boss* and *Facts of Life.* He was originally a musician who played in a popular Cairo orchestra.

Many Egyptians are making important contributions to their adopted country. Some are distinguished doctors, scientists, and engineers. Dr. Hossam Fadel was among the first physicians in the United States to work in the field of maternal fetal medicine, which is concerned with high-risk pregnancy. He founded the department of Maternal Fetal Medicine at the Medical College of Georgia. Dr. Magdi Yacoub, a heart surgeon, has pioneered heart and lung transplant techniques.

Arab-American Organizations

Over the years, some organizations have been set up in the United States to assist both new immigrants and established Arab Americans. One, the National Association of Arab Americans (NAAA), helps Egyptians and other Arabs adapt to life in the United States. It encourages its members to participate in social and political affairs. At the same time, the group tries to foster appreciation among Arab Americans for their cultural heritage. The NAAA also reaches out to promote friendship and cooperation between the United States and the Arab world.

Another prominent organization, the Arab American Institute, in Washington, D.C., works specifically to give Arab Americans political power. Its executive director, James Zogby, works with Arab-American communities around the nation. The AAI offers them leadership workshops that provide special training in skills like campaigning, party leadership, and developing closer ties with city and state governments. The workshops give participants a real sense of their own power to change society.

Many Egyptians and other Arab Americans would agree on one aspect of society that needs to change: ignorance and prejudice against Arabs. In American films and television, Arabs have historically been portrayed in a negative way. Depicted as untrustworthy and savage, they have been "the American Indians of the Middle East."

Despite efforts against stereotyping, prejudice against Arab Americans continues today. Frequently, all Arabs are suspected of being terrorists because some Arab terrorist groups are in the headlines. And during the recent war in the Persian Gulf, many radio stations across the United States played songs that not only made fun of and attacked Iraqi leader Saddam Hussein, but all Arabs as well. At that time, many Arab Americans were both offended and afraid. With the help of organizations like the NAAA and the AAI, ignorance and prejudice toward Arab Americans will be replaced by understanding, tolerance, and respect.

Will They Go Back?

Egyptians who come to the United states are generally pleased with their adopted country. They work hard to build new lives for their families. Unlike some other minority groups, Egyptians tend to become part of the fabric of their new nation. "We are really not like the Chinese, who continue their culture in America with Chinatowns. We tend to mix more," says one Egyptian immigrant.

"This is my home," the man continues. "I wouldn't go back." But then he remembers an old Egyptian proverb and smiles. "Anyone who has drunk the waters of the Nile returns to Egypt."

Appendix

Egyptian Embassies and Consulates in the United States and Canada

The Egyptian consulates in the United States and Canada want to help Americans and Canadians better understand Egypt. For more information about Egypt, contact the consulate or embassy nearest you.

U.S. Embassy and Consulates

Chicago, Illinois
Consulate General of the Arab Republic of Egypt
30 South Michigan Avenue
7th Floor
Chicago, IL 60603
Phone (312) 443–1190

Houston, Texas
Consulate General of the Arab Republic of Egypt
2000 West Loop South
Suite 1750
Control Data Building
Houston, TX 77027
Phone (713) 961–4915

New York, New York
Consulate General of the Arab Republic of Egypt
1110 Second Avenue
New York, NY 10022
Phone (212) 759–7120

Washington, D.C.
Embassy of the Arab Republic of Egypt
2310 Decatur Place, N.W.
Washington, D.C. 20008
Phone (202) 232–5400

Canadian Embassy

Ottawa, Canada
Embassy of the Arab Republic of Egypt
454 Laurier Avenue East
Ottawa, Ontario K1N 6R3
Canada
Phone (613) 234–4931

Glossary

Allah (AAH-la) — the Arabic name for God

Bedouin (BED-ou-in) — animal herders who move from place to place in the deserts of the Arab world, including Egypt

dynasty (DIE-ni-stee) — a series of rulers who belong to the same family

Eid al-Adha (eed-al-AHD-ha) — the Feast of the Sacrifice, celebrated during pilgrimage time

fellahin (fell-la-HEEN) — the peasant farmers who live and work in the Nile Valley

ful (FOOL) — the national dish, made of beans and spices

gallabiyyas (gal-a-BI-yas) — the flowing white gowns worn by Egyptian men

Hyksos (HICK-sohs) — a Semitic people, probably from Palestine, who conquered Egypt about 1725 B.C.

Islam (is-LAHM) — the Arabic word for "submission" to God. Islam is one of the world's great religions. Its members believe in one God, Allah, and his prophet, Muhammad.

jinn (GIN) — supernatural being popular in Arabic folklore

Koran (kor-AAN) — the sacred book of the Muslims

kuttab (coot-TAHB) — a religious school, usually in a mosque, where students study aspects of the Koran

Mamelukes (MAM-uh-lyooks) — non-Arab soldiers who rose from slavery and seized control of Egypt in A.D. 1250. They ruled for more than 250 years.

minaret (mih-nah-REHT) — a thin tower from which a caller (a muezzin) invites Muslims to prayer

mosque (MAHSK) — the Islamic place of public religious worship

muezzin (mu-EZ-in) — the caller in the minaret

Muhammad (moo-HAHM-ahd) — the Arab prophet (A.D. 570–632) who founded the religion of Islam

Muslim (MUHZ-luhm) — the Arabic word for "one who submits." A Muslim submits to Allah, or God, under the religion of Islam. Its members believe in one God.

prophet (PROF-it)—a person who spreads a message believed to come from God. Also, a person who tells what will happen in the future.

Ptolemy (TOL-eh-mee)—the name of the rulers of the Greek dynasty that ruled Egypt for nearly 300 years, from 323 B.C. to 30 B.C.

Ramadan (rah-mah-DAHN)—the Islamic month during which Muslims refrain from eating or drinking each day from dawn until sundown

sakieh (sa-KEE-ah)—the primitive water wheel still used by fellahin to irrigate the land

zabbaleen (za-bah-LEEN)—trash collectors in Cairo

Selected Bibliography

Abraham, Nicholas. *Doing Business in Egypt.* Boston: Tradeship Publishing, 1979.

Cross, Wilbur. *Enchantment of the World: Egypt.* Chicago: Children's Press, 1982.

El-Shamy, Hasan. *Folktales of Egypt.* Chicago: University of Chicago Press, 1980.

Feinstein, Stephen. *Egypt in Pictures.* Minneapolis: Lerner Publications Company, 1988.

Nelson, Nina. Egypt. London: B.T. Batsford, 1976.

Rugh, Andrea. *Family in Contemporary Egypt.* Syracuse: Syracuse University Press, 1984.

Siamon, Sharon and Jeff. *Children of Other Lands: Egypt.* Markham, Ont.: Grolier, 1990.

Von Haag, Michael. *Travelaid Guide to Egypt.* London: Travelaid Publishing, 1981.

Wilkins, Frances. *Let's Visit Egypt.* London: Burke Publishing Company, 1977.

Index

Africa, 8, 20, 41, 45
Alexander the Great, 47
Alexandria, 19, 20, 39, 47
"Ali Baba and the Forty Thieves," 63
Ali, Muhammad, 52, 53
Allah, 34
Amenhotep IV (Akhenaton), 45, 46
Arab American Institute (AAI), 119
Arabic, 38, 94, 98
Archemedes' screw, 26
Aswan High Dam, 15, 25
A Thousand and One Nights, 62
Aton, 45, 46

Bedouins, 25, 32, 33
belly dancing, 39
Bonaparte, Napolean, 51, 52
Britain, 41, 53, 54

Cairo, 7, 10, 15, 20, 21, 28, 39, 40
celebrations: Christmas Eve, 76; *Eid al-Fitr*, 73; Epiphany, 76; *Maulid al-Nabi*, 69; New Year's Eve, 76; *Ramadan*, 72; Seven-Day Party, 77; *Shem al-Nessim*, 68, 69
Christianity, 35, 50
Citadel, the, 52, 53, 73
City of the Dead, 28, 78
Cleopatra, 50
Coptic Orthodox Church, 35
Copts, 35, 76, 77
cotton, 16, 19

Dakhilah, 11

Early New Kingdom, 45
education:boys, for, 95; class trips, 98; cost of, 100; girls, for, 95;
higher education, 101; high school, 100; intermediate school, 99; language schools, 95; libraries for, 94; primary school, 95; private schools, 95; public schools, 95; school day, 97; teachers, role of, 98; tests, 99; tutoring, 100; uniforms, 97; women, for, 101
Egypt: children in, 69, 73, 81; climate of, 14; constitution of, 21; economy of, 17, 19; emigration from, 113; family life in, 78-84; folklore of, 59-65; foods of, 86-90; government of, 21-23; housing in, 20, 78, 79; immigration to, 24; industry in, 17; invasions of, 47-50; literary life of, 39; location of, 8; movies in, 40; museums in, 40; music in, 39; names for, 21; publishing in, 38; religion in, 34-38; size of, 8; traditional dress of, 33; women, roles of, 84, 85
el-arusa, 68
El Faiyum, 10, 11
el-Sadat, Anwar, 32, 55

Fadel, Dr. Hossam, 118
farmers, 15, 17, 23, 25
Farouk, King, 54
fellahin, 25, 27
First Intermediate Period, 44
France, 41, 51, 53

Gulf War, 57

Hatshepsut, 45
hookah, 29

About the Author

Arthur Diamond, born in Queens, New York, has lived and worked in Colorado, New Mexico, and Oregon. He received a Bachelor's degree in English from the University of Oregon and a Master's degree in English/Writing from Queens College.

Mr. Diamond is the author of several nonfiction books. A writer and teacher, he currently lives in his boyhood home with his wife, Irina, and their children, Benjamin Thomas and Jessica Ann.